Slow Dancing in
Emotional Minefields

BY

Tigranus Levantus

A K A

Ronald E. Frustaglia

Each individual piece has its own dedication but the book in its entirety is dedicated...

To JENNIFER LORI BONIN WHEN WE MET, I WAS LONG PAST LONELY AND LOST. YOU HELPED TO SAVE ME FROM MYSELF.

ALSO to MY DAUGHTER SHANNON PAYNE HOGAN BORN SHANNON PAYNE FRUSTAGLIA BECAUSE I HAVE LOVED YOU EVERY DAY OF YOUR LIFE AND I HAVE ALWAYS WISHED I COULD TELL WHY I HAD TO LEAVE.

AND ALSO to the memory of my friend JAMES CARCERANO WHO WAS known as JIMMY CASS. JIMMY WAS THE ONLY FRIEND I EVER HAD WHO BELIEVED THAT I COULD BE A WRITER AND BELIEVED THAT I HAD SOMETHING TO SAY. I MISS HIM. WE WERE FRIENDS FOR OVER FIFTY YEARS WHEN HE PASSED AWAY.

Contents

Acknowledgments

I would like to thank everyone in my life that encouraged me to write. Very few people in my life encouraged me.

Most people in my life tried to discourage me.

Some laughed and made fun of me.

Above all others I would like to thank FATHER FRANCIS SOLANUS my freshman ENGLISH teacher at CHRISTOPHER COLUMBUS CATHOLIC HIGH SCHOOL in BOSTON, MASSACHUSETTS.

FATHER FRANCIS was a tough teacher and a tough man. I remember him telling us that he was an intramural middleweight champ in THE UNITED STATES MARINE CORPS during the KOREAN WAR.

He assigned us one composition a week.

He said that it did not matter what it was about.

All he did say was that we needed to stretch our minds and find something to write about and that it must be one full page at least.

One full page equates to approximately 250 words.

This seemingly simple weekly assignment provided me with the inspiration and desire to be a writer.

I was thirteen years old.

Unfortunately those weekly compositions are residing in the slush pile of HISTORY. Oh! How I wish that I made copies of these compositions and kept them. Some were quite amusing.

HOWEVER, I did begin to write and I kept a large spiral notebook filled with the angst prose and FREE VERSE of an overfed, long-haired, arrogant, and lonely adolescent.

That notebook was burned by me long ago when I was fifteen years old because some neighborhood kids made fun of me when they stole the notebook and read what was inside.

It wasn't until twenty-five years later in 1997 that I became serious about becoming a writer

I write every day now based on a homework assignment all those years ago.

I write free-verse poetry, personal essays, AUTO-BIO-GRAPHICAL essays, short fiction, long fiction, and CRE-ATIVE NON-FICTION.

I may not be a published writer yet, but I can call myself a writer because I write every day after stretching my mind a bit.

Sadly, FATHER FRANCIS has long since died. If only I had the chance to tell him just how much he influenced my life. This is my most fervent wish.

I would like to also thank FATHER WILLIAM O. BERRY my junior and senior ENGLISH teacher at CHRISTOPHER COLUMBUS CATHOLIC HIGH SCHOOL in BOSTON MASSACHUSETTS.

FATHER WILLIAM gave me a love of literature that still resonates with me today.

I remember that he once said to me, "Read everything. Don't just read what you like. Sometimes you should read what you don't like or books that challenge the way you currently think. You may learn to hold two diametrically opposed thoughts in your head at the same time."

The last time I saw FATHER WILLIAM was in 1988. His final words to me were these: "Start with the ANCIENTS and work your way through HISTORY to the present day." The man was a sage and did not know it. I wish I knew what happened to FATHER WILLIAM.

I do not know if he is alive or dead.

I would also like to thank everyone in my life that told me I could never and would never be a writer.

Each and every one of those people will remain nameless because they do not matter.

I would also like to thank everyone who ever made fun of me and laughed at me. These people will also remain nameless because they do not matter. I thank these people because I became more and more determined to be a writer after each word of discouragement and derision.

I EXTEND SPECIAL THANKS TO JULIE CHARLES OF NORFOLK, VIRGINIA, MADELINE ALBANO OF BOSTON'S NORTH END, BERNA DINUNZIO OF BOSTON'S NORTH END, TONI ANN GUARINO OF BOSTON'S NORTH END, VILMA DIFRONZO, OF BOSTON'S NORTH END, AND THE CARDONE FAMILY – STEPHANIE, BUNNI, BIG VIC, AND LITTLE VIC OF BOSTON'S NORTH END.

AND, FOR THE LAST A VERY SPECIAL THANK YOU TO AUTUMN ROSE LUTHARDT OF NORFOLK, VIRGINIA. YOUR TWIN GIFTS OF FORGIVENESS AND FRIENDSHIP MEAN MORE TO ME THAN YOU COULD POSSIBLY KNOW.

And a very special thank you goes to a childhood friend FRANK TERRANOVA.

I also would like to thank the PANTHEON of my heroes.

The Pantheon of My Heroes

All of these men and women are heroes not only to me but to millions. All of these men and women have also inspired me to strive for excellence in thought and deed. Each member of the PANTHEON of my HEROES has provided me with inspiration, determination, and encouragement by the example of their accomplishments in life.

I am forever grateful to their memory.

WINSTON CHURCHILL: CHURCHILL influenced me because he showed the world that through sheer force of anything can be accomplished.

JOHN FITZGERALD KENNEDY: JFK influenced me and brought my idealism to the forefront of my thoughts.

ROBERT FRANCIS Kennedy: RFK influenced me because of his ability to bring disparate groups together in common cause.

MARTIN LUTHER KING JR: DOCTOR KING influenced me because he had a dream that inspired me to dream.

ERNEST HEMINGWAY: HEMINGWAY influenced me because his prose was simple and powerful. For the most part his life was also an inspiration. We'll skip the suicide part.

GORE VIDAL: VIDAL'S work inspires me to strive for excellence in the world of the ESSAYIST and the world of the HISTORICAL NOVELIST. In my opinion VIDAL is one of the three greatest writers of the TWENTIETH CENTURY. The other two being ERNEST HEMINGWAY and JOHN STEINBECK.

JOHN STEINBECK: Steinbeck influenced me through his work and the messages his work conveyed. His main themes in my opinion were fate and injustice where the downtrodden and the ordinary man finds himself trying to live with everything against him. His NOVELLAS become more DEAR TO ME AS I READ AND RE-READ THEM WITH REGULARITY. He inspires me because of his outstanding social perception. I need to get better at this.

ALLEN GINSBURG: GINSBURG and all of the other beats influenced me and continue to inspire me because they all changed the way literature is written and read. GINSBURG especially was a large influence and inspiration because his work spoke to me and it said that it is okay to be different and to show the world who and what you really are and it is okay to howl your dissatisfaction with how things are and to shout your feelings to the masses saying what you are for and against. Because of GINSBURG I know that my path is to HOWL AND SCREAM at the prosecution and persecution of the powerless.

ROD MCKUEN: MCKUEN influenced and inspired me through his marvelous use of the ENGLISH LANGUAGE, especially his titles. My favorite being LISTEN TO THE WARM.

BRUCE SPRINGSTEEN: I first heard BRUCE SPRING-STEEN in 1974. I was seventeen years old. I couldn't believe what I was hearing. The music was enthralling and riveting. The lyrics were captivating and intense. I was hooked from that moment on. I am still a fan to my core. That first song was ROSA-LITA. BRUCE SPRINGSTEEN became a major influence and inspiration in my life from the first moment I heard his words and music. He spoke to me and we have had a one-way conversation since then. He speaks for the disaffected, the disenchanted, and the disgruntled. He is the champion of the workingman and the everyman. I strive to do the same with my writing. His writing isn't just poetic. It is prophetic and it is food for those who are starving for meaning in their lives. He truly is "THE BOSS." He brings to bear the struggles of everyday life.

JOHN LENNON: JOHN LENNON influenced and inspired me through his lyrics and his relentless belief in activism advocating for PEACE and because he truly was a working-class hero. I still miss him.

DESMOND DOSS: I knew of DESMOND DOSS long before the movie HACKSAW RIDGE came out. DOSS is a hero, influence, and inspiration because he stayed true to his beliefs under the most horrific conditions imaginable. He never once wavered. I only hope that I can follow his example.

ALLAN TURING: Long before the movie, THE IMITATION GAME was released. I entered Turing into my pantheon of heroes HE is an inspiration because he played such a pivotal part in the allied victory in WORLD WAR TWO. It is estimated that his efforts shortened the war in EUROPE by nearly two years and saved about FOURTEEN MILLION lives. He influenced me by confirming the simple fact that one man's intellect and efforts can make a difference in any undertaking.

ELEANOR ROOSEVELT: MRS. ROOSEVELT is one of the few people in history that can be described as a force of nature. MRS ROOSEVELT is an influence and inspiration because of her many firsts and her dedication to human rights, equal rights and civil rights.

CLAUDETTE COLVIN: MISS COLVIN is a hero, an inspiration, and an influence on me because 9 months prior to ROSA PARKS she refused to give up her seat on the bus to a white man. COLVIN WAS a 15-YEAR-OLD girl with enough courage to help launch a movement that would change history. COURAGE and BRAVERY are 2 words that are grossly overused these days, but they are fitting for MISS COLVIN. As a 15 year old girl she should have been dreaming about pretty dresses and handsome boys but there she was in the very forefront of history. Her actions only seek to prove that one person can change the world that he or she lives in. MISS COLVIN, I applaud and venerate your life.

ROSA PARKS: Because of CLAUDETTE COLVIN, ROSA PARKS and DOCTOR KING. The CIVIL RIGHTS MOVEMENT OF THE 1950'S AND 1960'S took off and changed the way we lived. Again, this is proof that one person can change the way we think and feel. These three people will continue to influence and inspire me until I breathe my last.

HARVEY MILK: HARVEY MILK believed that no sacrifice is too great if laid at the altar of HUMAN RIGHTS. HARVEY MILK is an inspiration and an influence because of his immense courage and his devotion to the cause of HUMAN RIGHTS.

AUGUSTA CHIWY – THE FORGOTTEN ANGEL OF BASTOGNE: AUGUSTA CHIWY was without a doubt the bravest individual on the planet. She was born in the BELGIAN CONGO. Her father was a Belgian veterinarian and her mother was a native CONGOLESE woman. In BELGIUM SHE TRAINED as a NURSE WHEN SHE WAS NINETEEN YEARS OLD. In 1944 during the BATTLE OF THE BULGE near her hometown of BASTOGNE she volunteered at an aid station. She would frequently traverse the battlefields in an ARMY UNIFORM to retrieve wounded soldiers at great risk to herself. These selfsame soldiers that she saved and treated heaped racial slurs, invective, and abuse upon her until the aid station DOCTOR put an end to it by telling the soldiers that she treats you or you die. Her courage and bravery inspires and influences me by giving me a template on how a HUMAN BEING should act.

OSKAR SCHINDLER: If the movie about his life is even a little accurate. SHINDLER is a hero to the world. He saved a generation of JEWS. He remains an influence and inspiration to me because of his willingness to give everything he had to save lives.

DALTON TRUMBO: TRUMBO IS AN INFLUENCE AND INSPIRATION because he was able to stand by the courage of his convictions and refused to testify against his Hollywood colleagues in 1947 AT HUAC – THE HOUSE UNAMERICAN ACTIVITIES COMMITTEE led by SENATOR MCCARTHY. As a result he became one of the HOLLYWOOD TEN who were blacklisted. TRUMBO sacrificed his career and livelihood but found ways to keep working by using pseudonyms and fronts. He even managed to win two ACADEMY AWARDS WHILE BLACKLISTED. Of course he was unable to receive credit for his work or accept the awards. Trumbo's perseverance is an example to everyone. To me TRUMBO is an example of honor and integrity. He NEVER SURRENDERED AND HE NEVER RETREATED EVEN THOUGH BEING BLACKLISTED COST HIM EVERYTHING.

KIRK DOUGLAS: DOUGLAS is an inspirational and influential hero because it was his unselfish act and sense of moral integrity that helped put an end to a dark period in the history of THE UNITED STATES OF AMERICA. HE was a pivotal player in ending the HOLLYWOOD BLACKLIST in 1960 by giving DALTON TRUMBO an on-screen credit for his screenplay of SPARTACUS. By doing this DOUGLAS put his Hollywood career and his personal wealth at risk.

DORIE MILLER: PETTY OFFICER MILLER was a MESSMAN in THE UNITED STATES NAVY. I was also a MESSMAN in THE U.S. NAVY. MILLER is a hero, an influence, and an inspiration because of his courage under fire, His presence of mind, his strength of character, and his ability to rise above those who would keep him down. DORIE MILLER is my idea of what a hero should be. He is an icon to AFRICAN AMERICANS and all AMERICANS.

IRENE SENDLER: MS. SENDLER is a hero, an influence, and an inspiration to me because she gave her life in a HUMANITARIAN effort to save JEWISH children from the WARSAW GHETTO IN WORLD WAR TWO.

PINCHAS ROSENBAUM: ROSENBAUM was a HUNGARIAN JEW who saved thousands of his people from the NAZI death camps by masquerading as an officer in the SS and also by disguising himself as an officer in the ARROW CROSS PARTY WHICH WAS SYMPATHETIC TO HITLER. ROSENBAUM risked his life daily for others.

CAPTAIN FRANK REGINALD BECK OF THE SANDRINGHAM COMPANY OF VOLUNTEERS. BECK MOLDED A GROUP OF FARM LABORERS, GROOMS FOOTMEN AND STABLE HANDS INTO A VIABLE FIGHTING UNIT THAT SERVED AT THE BATTLE OF GALLIPOLI. THEY DISAPPEARED INTO LEGEND.

Preface

I argue that modern poetry except for lyrics to popular songs should be devoid of rhyme and meter. I also argue that the writer of modern poetry should not write in an historical vacuum. The poet must strive to create verse that is relevant to the times he or she writes in as well as trying to maintain relevancy in HIS or HER writing for future generations. The poetry that fills this book is modern in scope. It is free verse. When I say FREE VERSE, I mean that it is free of the constraints of METER, RHYME, CONSISTENT PATTERNS, rules of GRAMMAR and punctuation. BUT, according to the AMERICAN critic JOHN LIVINGSTON LOWES in 1916 FREE VERSE may be written as beautiful PROSE while PROSE may be written as beautiful FREE VERSE. Which is which? SO, herein lays a conundrum. While I am not smart enough to sort out and/or solve this CONUNDRUM I hope that the work you – my dear gentle reader – read here will be a flowing rhythm of words that will make you stop and think, pause and ponder your world as well as mine. But, above all my goal is to make you more aware of the life inside and all around you. I also strive to document the human condition.

Introduction

PAT BENATAR, AN 80'S ROCK'N'ROLLER and her song-writing partner and guitarist NEIL GERALDO said, "LOVE is a battlefield". Based on that statement I say that all of life is a battlefield. Because, LIFE is the search for LOVE. Thank you, MISS BENATAR, but you neglected to mention that the battlefield was salted and peppered with EMOTIONAL MINE-FIELDS. AND, that those minefields were filled with both wonder and treachery.

EMOTIONS rule our waking lives so consequently mines are exploding all around us when we are afraid or frightened or scared. The same goes for feelings of anger, sadness, joy, love, happiness, despair, and exultation. Emotional shrapnel surrounds us all.

Author's Note to the Reader

Each poem is a separate story. In this work the phrase this POET can also be read as the PRONOUN I. I consider myself a CONFESSIONALIST POET writing in free verse. My work is highly personal and deals with the psychology of the self because much of this work is somewhat autobiographical in nature if not in experience. I also consider myself a poet in the MODERNIST STYLE.

Slow Dancing in Emotional Minefields

Where Do Broken Dreams Go?

For Harry Chapin

There are times when this poet just sits wondering
when the next word will come.
He sits Thinking about
where he will place that word.
He reflects on
what he has already written.

He then tries to figure out if
HARRY CHAPIN knew of the place when he asked
Where do broken dreams go?
This poet thinks that broken dreams
find their way to a dark corner of memory waiting to be
dreamt again.
How sad the poet says to himself.

This poet doesn't dream anymore.
Dreaming is too painful.

He just remembers his dreams
with a sense of melancholy
and longing of
what it was like to dream the dreams
he used to dream.
The poet now dreams about his faded hopes, foggy aspirations,
and shadowy wishes.

Sometimes this poet just sits motionless
in a dark room with the window shades down
and curtains closed to shut out the world
giving him a sense of freedom from himself.
He knows that he has to be comfortable
with his own thoughts.

He is listening for what he cannot understand just yet
and he doesn't know what those dreams may be
and again he wonders where do broken dreams go?
Is it possible that broken dreams are hiding in plain sight?
Or, have they gone away forever?
Will the poet learn to dream again?
Sometimes he just sits,
waiting anxiously for something to happen.
And the poet wonders once again.
Where do broken dreams go?
And, will he find some words to ease his suffering?
Are the dreams really gone?
The optimist in the poet says
They have manifested themselves into something else.
But what have they become he asks himself?
He hasn't a clue.
The pessimist in him says they are irretrievable.
Has life beaten him down?
It Seems so.

Sometimes he just sits alone pondering and wondering if
Harry Chapin was right after all?
Are you supposed to dream only when you're young?

Casualty: A Letter Home from the Western Front

This is inspired by THE WAR POETS AND TWO MOVIES THE FIRST MOVIE BEING REGENERATION AND THE SECOND MOVIE BEING ALL THE KINGS MEN. REGENERATION is a story about two war poets being treated for shellshock in a hospital. ALL THE KINGS MEN IS THE STORY OF CAPTAIN FRANK BECK.

THIS IS FOR THE SHOCKED AND SHATTERED

My Dearest,
Your last letter brought me much joy.
I must push that joy from my mind
because it is torture
to think about you and our girls MILLICENT and CECILY
while there is so much
blood and carnage all around me.
Love and comfort have no place here.
Hope is a luxury that I can ill afford
as it is pounded to dust from all of the shelling.
My life is confined to the trenches
where the gardens of home have been replaced
with barbed wire as far as the eye can see.
This is my last letter to you and the girls because.

Soon, I'll be coming home from this wretched war.

This war is nothing like
what my father told me that war should be.
This war is nothing like
what I learned in school.
Here there is no honor.
Here there are no rules.
Here there are no gentlemen.
Here there is only pain and suffering
on such a massive scale that it
scant seems possible but it truly is so
mired in anguish and melancholy.

I have seen so much blood.
Pain is all pervasive.
Bodies litter the vast spaces
of what is called no-man's land.
Bodies are draped on the barbed wire
that separates us from the enemy
Blood sparkles in the early morning light
when it bounces off of our tin pot helmets.

My heart is full of anger and hate
that men should do the things they do to their fellow men.

and my feet are full of sores from
Marching to the massacres I've witnessed
and taken part in.

In the minds of the young men who are fighting
this wretched war
there is nothing left but madness
because of the incessant shelling all around us.
Dawn is never quiet,
neither is dusk.

And in myself I find
that the madness has invaded and infected my mind.

I ask the doctors and the generals
what we have done.

Why is the price so high?
WE have lost an entire generation.
I weep for our future as a civilization.

I received no answers from the doctors or the generals.
I only received looks of incredulity
that I had the bald-faced audacity, the temerity,
and the unmitigated gall
to ask such questions of my betters.

It would appear that the only men left
are shell-shocked and shattered.
They have been reduced to empty vessels devoid of humanity,
but they are lucky to be alive,
or are they?

These young men
still have their bodies
But their souls and minds have long SINCE deserted them
Here there is no dignity
while standing in water that is knee deep
while quite literally defecating ourselves to death.

There is no such thing as a lucky man here.

But I cannot be so sure.
I trust that this final missive from the front
finds you and our girls healthy.
I am not the same man that you remember.
I am broken but with some care
I hope to recover and mend.

It will take me many a long year
to return to any semblance of normality.
But, with you at my side to keep me warm and safe beside you
I know that I can overcome anything.
Love to you and the girls.
I am forever your PERCIVAL.

A Death Song

Inspired by the samurai

For those in need of a reason to believe

I am like the samurai of feudal JAPAN
in that the SAMURAI composes a death poem.
Unlike the samurai
this poet has no intention of committing suicide.

As he sleeps
He prays that the darkness
Will bring an end to his suffering.
As the POET sleeps
He prays that death
Will come to take him
to the place that we go when we die
wherever that place may be.
He prays but he doesn't believe in any god.
HE wonders if it is of any use to pray.
Maybe there is a reason to pray
because nothing made of matter
ever really dies because my dear reader
the universe recycles everything.
The poet wants to die.
He believes that his reason for living is gone.

He doesn't want to face another day.
But, a new day dawns as if to spite him
His will to live is gone as if it dissipated
in the winds of pain and anguish.
The fire is gone from his eyes.
Words are difficult to come by
and when they do come to him,
they are meaningless
because desire and will have faded from his life.
His inner spirit has deserted him,
The essence of life is missing from his being.
All this happened because
He loved a woman too much.
She didn't love him back.
He lost himself in his love for her.
He fears the loneliness that is coming upon him.
He cannot find meaning or purpose in life anymore.
He believes that he cannot face another day.
But life has a way of restoring
meaning, purpose, and love.
Time and patience are the answers to all things.
Oh my how cliché is this?

He is ashamed of himself but there is no shame in death.
There is no shame in wanting death.
His shame is from weakness.
His weakness is from fighting
too many emotional battles and he is tired.
As slivers of light peek through his bedroom window
he wakes hoping to find the courage to stop wishing for death
and to begin anew.
The poet forgets that there is always hope.
And, hope is a good thing.
It is one thing that nobody but oneself can take away

On the Day After

This is for everyone who has loved and lost

*This is dedicated to Jen Bonin, Stephanie Cardone, Bunni
Cardone, the memory of Little Victor Cardone and the
memory of Big Victor Cardone*

On the day after
I die
Do not bury me.
Place me in a cheap wooden box
and put the box on a pyre.
Light the pyre and burn me.
Collect my ashes and place them in an empty wine bottle.
Empty the bottle onto the surf of any ocean
On the day after
My ashes are scattered into the sea
Take the empty bottle to the end of the pier
on LEWIS WHARF in BOSTON and throw the bottle
into the sea. It is then that you must play a song by
NEIL DIAMOND for me.
Please play I AM. I SAID.
On the day after
My soul AND SPIRIT begin its ride
upon the wind and I become a memory
Look beside you on your left and then your right.
Then Look behind you
I will always be there.
Only the body dies.
MEMORIES ARE ETERNAL.

Onward Middle Class Soldiers

For those who struggle to find life's meaning

They stumble towards apathy.
The rich keep getting richer
and the poor are clamoring for justice
because they keep getting poorer.

The middle class if there ever was one
and the working poor class are still waiting for trickle – down
economics to work.
It seems as if they will be waiting forever.
Their eyes fill with tears at the ever-widening gulf of prosperity
between the haves and the have nots.

They drift through a region of uncertainty
Falling over the rocks of empty promises that
Shattered their dreams and fractured their hopes.

They groan with false hopes
in their belief that the government will fix them.
Their backs are bent under ever-increasing burdens.

"When will our time come?" they wonder.

"Who will be our champion?" they cry OUT.
Is there no one who will help us?
MILTON FRIEDMAN LIED.
REAGAN LIED.

BUSH LIED AND SO DID HIS SON.
THE FOUNDING FATHERS LIED.

Will the AMERICAN DREAM ever become a reality
or is it dead and buried?
Will AMERICA ever live up to its promises and its creed?
I think not
Greed governs
along with the unenlightened and grotesque gurus of self-interest.

Did THE AMERICAN DREAM
ever exist in the first place?

OR, did the lies start at the very beginning of
THE AMERICAN EXPERIMENT?

In His Name?

For the misguided

Inspired by Emerson, Lake, and Palmer

He lay
Bleeding and dying
BY a stream
IN A GLORIOUSLY GREEN MEADOW.
He was whispering the secret names of god,
but he never did believe in imaginary friends.

He had hoped that there was a GOD
so that he could be forgiven
for killing in his name.

And, all the while as he waited for DEATH
to claim him, he cried.

For him, there was no forgiveness.
There can be no SALVATION for a WARRIOR-PRIEST.
A man cannot have two masters.
For him there was no redemption.
For him there would be no peace.

Sidewalk Sidestep

For the homeless heroes

SUMMER 1980
KENMORE SQUARE,
BOSTON, MASSACHUSETTS

He died early one morning.
He collapsed in front of a crowd
of revelers none of whom came forward to help.
He was drunk and he was sick.
He smelled of death.
He was alone.
He had no home, no friends,
and no comfort of any kind
He had nothing but memories
that haunted him.
His spirit was crushed
beneath the weight of injustice
There was nobody to mourn him.
The revelers just stepped to the right
of the mess on the sidewalk that was once a proud man
and a hero.

Then, one of the late-night revelers came forward
and laid his coat over the man.
Someone in the crowd WENT TO A PAYPHONE
ON THE CORNER
AND called the police emergency line.
Soon the area was then cordoned off to foot traffic.
A policeman bent over the body
and removed the covering of the coat of the kind reveler.
The police officer's eyes began to tear up
as he noticed a tattoo on the dead man's arm.
The tattoo was a globe and anchor.
The man who laid his coat over the body came forward
to the police officer.
He said. I noticed it as well.
He was a brother MARINE.
The police officer and the man both rolled up their sleeves
to bare their own tattoos
to honor their fallen brother.
At the same time they said to each other.
We have to do something.
They both cried in silence.
When enough tears were shed,
they rose as one and yelled as one.
Goodbye brother
rest easy.
We have the watch now.

In the Middle of the Garden of the Mind

For those who need help but fear asking

Once,
In the middle of the garden of my mind,

THERE stood A SOLITARY TREE
With many branches.

Each branch is a representation of the decisions
we make in our lives.
There are many leaves on the branches.
Each leaf represents a person in our lives.
People come and go.
It is in the spring that the leaves blossom.
In the fall the leaves fall to the ground.
Above a rosebush in another part of this garden
A bird sings to its mate
In a voice that glitters with longing.
Now,
In the middle of the garden of my mind
I sit laughing at the barrenness I see.
It is always winter here in my mind.
My feelings are like dead trees
swaying in a frigid breeze,
Cold and numb.

Silence Is an Executioner

For those who died from indifference

Silence tastes
Like a bitter root of despair
Silence feels like a warm breeze
containing a rush of disasters
Silence smells like the sea at night
before it rains
Silence looks like dimly lit shadows
On city streets
It grows within me becoming a companion, A friend,
and an executioner
The silence of despair, pain, anguish, and loneliness
Can be as lethal and effective executioner
as the guns of AUGUST in 1914
Silence in the heart
and silence in the brain
can shatter a man's mind with the same effectiveness as a
baseball bat to the head.
Silence is fearful to mankind.
If there is injustice in the world it is the silence
of good men doing nothing that
brings fear and misery to all of mankind
for the world is my country and all of mankind are my brethren.

Fear Is My Friend

For anyone who ever had to live in fear

Fear can paralyze you into inaction.
Fear can also galvanize you into action.
FEAR LETS ME KNOW IF I SHOULD MAKE A STAND
AND FIGHT OR IF I SHOULD TAKE FLIGHT.
Fear is a contradictory emotion.
Fear is a complex emotion as it is difficult to define.
There are many types of fear
Total, partial, and abject
Fear can consume you and rob you of the will to live
Fear can take on many forms.
There is fear of failure.
There is fear of success.
There is fear of having nothing to say.
There is fear of saying too much and becoming irrelevant.
There is fear of violence.
There is fear of how you react to violence heaped upon you.
There is fear of the future.
There is fear of the past.
Fear can also be a form of self-pity
Pain sometimes is a frequent companion of fear.
Pain is also a friend.
Pain lets you know you are still alive
I am so tired
But I cannot sleep
I fear what may happen
in my dreams and because of this

I lay awake until I cannot bear the rewinding
of the tapes of my life that keep playing on a loop in my brain
I laugh aloud
But I am not happy.
There is fear of happiness.
There is fear of moroseness.
I cry silently.
I am afraid of nothing.
I AM AFRAID Of everything
Fear is my friend
There are many kinds of fear.
And I experience them all at once.

Tears of Acid Rain

For all who loved, and lost without being loved back

Spring, 1997,
In the HIGH Desert of NEW MEXICO
at the place where a mushroom cloud once blossomed
because man decided to build a weapon to end civilization
as we know it.

The acid rain falls from clouds
in a blood and reddish orange sky a single raindrop flows
and trickles down my face
forming small furrows down my cheeks to my chin.
I scream your name aloud
to a faceless and invisible crowd.
I ask you why you threw me away.
Of course I receive no answer.
I have cried enough tears over you.
I will cry no more.
I am better off in my life without you.
My voice is hard to hear as it cracks and groans
The salt of the sands cripples and diminishes it.

Instead my voice whispers and whimpers
as I cry out in a pain
brought on by the agony of lost grace.

The Acid in the rain of tears
burns all the way through my skin where it stays
and finds my heart
devoid of compassion.
From my nose the teardrops slip
into a place inside my mouth where they are decimating
my screams.
I have no one to blame but myself.
My eyes close and I try to stop crying.
The shattering, chattering and blistering heat of the tears
form a Reflecting haze of the shimmering desert sands
that Wilts and disfigures my facial features and forms
cracks on my lips.
There once was a young man in this old face.
He was never really young though.
Now there is an older man in an older face.
He yearns for a day without the heat of hurt.
The tears ebb, slowly, into a drip,
A trickle that overflows again and overwhelms me
Once more as I sob and teeter, clumsily; without form
and feature.

I part my lips and grab my tongue
to stop the sounds of heartache and loneliness from
involuntarily escaping.

A scream Erupts from inside of me
turning into a shout of primal pain

My throat closes tight and fights off the sting of shame.
I want to hide from these Tears of Acid Rain,
but, in the desert you are naked. There is nowhere to hide.
My screams die with reluctance and the tears stop burning.

Now, as the sky turns from its blood red orange hue to a
blissful azure and baby blue.
I've forgotten your name.
It withered away and sailed across the desert on a
whispering wind.
I see echoes of a LED ZEPPELIN song.

Hope

For anyone who had hope and threw it away

ALEXANDER POPE
Once wrote of Hope.
Hope is a dangerous thing
because it comes with a false sense of security.

POPE said that hope springs eternal.
To me it's just infernal.
In me, it's dashed.
In me, it's smashed.
But if I ever again get a feeling of Hope,
I'll tie it with a Rope.
I don't know what drove the hope from me.
When I figure that out it is possible that I may once again be me.

Election Day

For all of us because we are all different and unique.

Sometime In the not too distant future
when white men of European descent and heritage are no
longer in the majority

An election day will come and go

Where a left-handed, red-haired, lesbian dwarf
Of color with violet eyes
Whose heritage is a mixture of hyphenated-Americans
Native indigenous, African, and Asian

Will be elected to a high office

And we will not think it unusual;
in fact, some of us will wonder why it took so long.

I hope that I live to see that day.

An Ordinary Man

For all of us who are not exceptional

He was an ordinary man.
He was small and insignificant.
He dreamed big dreams
He was deluded in his belief
that a man could be anything he chooses to be.

As small and insignificant as he was,
he dreamed big dreams
but those dreams were dashed against the hard rocks of reality
in this life.

In time this little man came to realize
that the extraordinary was beyond his grasp.
He began to write because he felt that writing was something
that ordinary men could succeed at.
He was trying to write great words to set other ordinary men's
souls ablaze
with a desire to dream extraordinary things
and to encourage other ordinary men to spit in the face of life
before life smacks them down.

HE Wrote that if ordinary men came together
for a single purpose they would be invincible.
With words these little, insignificant, and ordinary men
could shake the very foundation of conventional wisdom
and change what others believed them to be.

Little kindnesses and little acts of compassion
are the province of these ordinary men
Other men both high and low will sit up and take notice
of the compassion and kindness the little and insignificant
men exude.

They would rather be little, insignificant, and ordinary
than be born privileged.
The privileged are haughty and selfish and care not for the
most unfortunate in our society.
The underprivileged believe that kindness, compassion,
and selflessness is the path to greatness,
and this is how it should be.
This is the song of those ordinary men.
I want to sing my song for the world
I am an ordinary man
I am just an average JOE.
MY song is the song of the EVERYMAN.
My song is a song of TRIUMPH.
My song is a song of WHAT IF.

It begins I have hopes.
I have dreams.
I have lofty ambitions and aspirations.

I sing of living an ordinary life.
Take away the ordinary lives of ordinary men
And the bricks of civilization shatter.

Take away the ordinary man
And the mortar of life crumbles away.

On Sale Now

For the gullible

On sale now
For a limited time only
Forgiveness for all – only $79.95.
Redemption slashed to its lowest price
Of the holiday season – only $149.95.
Your prayers answered a bargain at – only $19.95.
Hurry!
Call now!
Use your credit card and
Receive a free gift with every order.
Supplies are limited.
Healing services not included.

I'm Going Home:
But You Can't Go Home Again:
Summer 2001

The houses have changed owners.
The shops have changed names.
I don't recognize anyone.
Nobody recognizes me.
I've been away a long time.
I've come home
But everyone I knew is
Gone or changed.
Nothing is the same
Except maybe me.
BUT Did I ever belong here?

Alone With Only My Thoughts

For the lonely

SPRING 2000
HURT, VIRGINIA

Alone,
At night,
In my basement bedroom
Without any windows,
I think.
I can't stop myself.
The tapes of my life are
in a constant state of re-wind and play-back.
They intertwine themselves with the tapes of history.
They intersperse themselves with tapes of old movies.
And then, the soundtrack starts. I can't stop it.
I can't control it.
I can't choose what scenes I want to see.
I can't choose what songs to hear.
Memories, good and bad, blend together in a nightmarish
and noirish montage.
The darkness of my room was once a friend.
I felt warm and safe in its enveloping softness.
But now, the darkness is a fiendish hellion.
Cold and cruel like a scorned lover,
the darkness laughs at my discomfort.
It rejoices at my fear.
It exults in my torment.

Co-Existence

Inspired by the movie Il Postino

For Pablo Neruda and Mario Ruopolo

I dedicate this to those who struggle to find poetry within themselves

NOTES TO THE READER:
Co-existence among people, cultures, faiths, countries, and civilizations is the key to the survival and advancement of humanity.
We are doomed if we do not find a way to live together in peace.
We are also doomed as a species if we do not embrace love, kindness, compassion, and diversity.

The storms had abated.
The winds blowing across the sea from the SAHARA HAD BEEN MURDEROUS.
Some of the fishermen were driven mad
by the screeching sounds of the SCIROCCO winds.
The winds were now quiet.
The sea was relatively calm but a tiny bit choppy.
But it was a workable sea once again.
A group of fishermen tried to untangle their nets.
The storms had tangled and twisted
all of the nets together
into a MODERN-DAY GORDIAN KNOT.

A fisherman with a small and pleading voice cried out.
        This is hopeless.
We will never be able to untangle these nets.

All of the rest mumbled their agreement except one.
A shrill and pleading voice called out.

        Why not sew the nets together?
The mumbling grew louder.
They looked at each other.
They were puzzled and befuddled.
Understanding and common sense escaped them.

Microcosm

For the unfortunates and homeless everywhere

Summer 1982
BOSTON, MASSACHUSETTS
A SOFT gentle SUMMER wind
Quite unlike the wind FRANK SINATRA sang about.
This wind heralded pain and suffering.
It is a wind that fans the dull brown
Concrete, steel, and glass haze of the city.
There is a waxing moon
that Shines on the high
Above glass and steel towers.
of rich and powerful men.
Two Shadows stir
on the steps of the city's library.

Day old newspapers and the accumulated detritus
of the city
skip across the gutters of the streets
The swirling front pages of the newspapers are dancing and
fluttering between the buildings.
All of the newspaper headlines shout of a booming economy.
A runaway in a tattered plaid skirt and
A wino in a frayed striped jacket descend the steps of the library.
They share a treat in the form of thrown away leftovers
in a paper bag from
A nearby garbage can.

these unfortunates are oblivious to the
Index of Leading Economic Indicators
On the front page of a financial publication shuffling by.

The clubs are closing.
Across the street is an all-night diner.
There in front of the diner THE late-night mating dance begins.
The beautiful people of the night sneer and avoid the
unfortunates in
A chorus of revulsion.
They don't see someone's daughter.

They don't see somebody's father or brother
or a war veteran and hero.
They stand aloof and contemptuous
Content in common disgust.
They secretly shudder in fear and loathing
like the pseudo intellectuals that they are.
The unfortunates cross the street and approach
the beautiful people to ask for spare change.

The so-called beautiful people scatter
as if a communicable disease was fast approaching them.
Kindness and compassion do not exist in the hearts of these
self-absorbed people
who are considered the beautiful people.
They don't realize that their society is judged by the way
that they treat our most unfortunate and disadvantaged citizens.
This poet weeps for the future.

Spring 1992: One Night at Chix Beach

For Julie Charles

It was a perfect night.
The summer breeze was skimming along the folds
of your dress.
The stars were lighting up your eyes in such a way
that accentuated your mischievous smile.
THE music was in our hearts,
but it spilled out onto our lips as we kissed so softly that it hurt.
Our love whistled its way through the trees ACROSS THE ROAD.
We held each other so tight that our arms ached.

Stolen Glances

For Berna Dinunzio and Donna Fantasia

WE WOULD GATHER WITH FRIENDS AT
DONNA'S HOUSE.
WE TALKED THROUGHOUT THE TWILIGHT HOURS
WHILE LISTENING TO MUSIC.
I ALWAYS HAD MY HEAD DOWN
LOOKING AT THE FLOOR
BUT I WOULD STEAL A GLANCE AT THE TWO OF
YOU SOMETIMES.
I COULD NEVER FIND THE COURAGE
TO TELL EITHER OF YOU HOW I FELT.
I NOW HAVE THE COURAGE BUT IT'S TOO LATE.
I LOVED YOU BOTH THEN AND I LOVE YOU
BOTH STILL.
I HOPE I CAN CALL YOU MY FOREVER FRIENDS.

I Chased You Away

For Toni Ann Guarino

I USED TO WAIT IN JOE FISH'S CLUB EVERY DAY
ALWAYS HOPING TO SEE YOU AND TALK TO YOU.
I ASKED YOU OUT SO MANY TIMES
THAT I CHASED YOU AWAY FROM ME.

Prom Night

For Vilma Difronzo

WHEN ROSE AND GERALD DROVE AWAY,
I GOT AFRAID.
I DIDN'T WANT THE NIGHT TO END.
I WALKED YOU UP THE STEPS
AND GENTLY HUGGED YOU.
WE EXCHANGED A CHASTE KISS
BUT IT STILL TOOK MY BREATH AWAY.
I WANTED TO SAY SOMETHING
BUT AT THAT MOMENT YOUR MOTHER
OPENED THE DOOR.
I ONLY WISH THAT I HAD SAID THOSE THREE
MAGIC WORDS TO YOU.
I COULD SAY THEM NOW
BUT I'M OVER FORTY YEARS TOO LATE.

EVERY TIME I LOOKED AT YOU,
I HAD TO STOP AND CATCH MY BREATH.
IT WAS THE MOST JOYOUS NIGHT OF MY LIFE.
I FELT LIKE I WAS DREAMING IN STEREO.
YOU WERE SO LOVELY IN YOUR BLUE DRESS.
YOUR FATHER WAS SO FUNNY
WHEN HE GAVE ME HIS TIE
BECAUSE HE SAID IT MATCHED YOUR DRESS.

Sharing an Evening of Music

For Madeline Albano

YOU INVITED ME INTO YOUR HOME
I WONDERED WHY YOU
TOOK PITY ON ME.
THE KIDS AT THE CLUB MADE FUN OF ME
AND LAUGHED AT ME BUT YOU DIDN'T.
I KNOCKED ON THE DOOR AND YOU LET ME IN
AND SAID COME INTO MY ROOM.
WE SAT ON THE FLOOR LOOKING THROUGH
YOUR ALBUMS
AND FINALLY CHOOSING ONE
IT WAS DEJA VU BY CROSBY, STILLS, NASH & YOUNG.
YOU PUT IT ON THE RECORD PLAYER
WE SAT ON THE FLOOR.
WE TALKED ABOUT MUSIC FOR HOURS
AFTERWARDS.
WHEN I SAID I HAD TO GO HOME
YOU WALKED ME TO THE DOOR.
I QUIETLY SAID I LOVE YOU
BUT YOU DIDN'T HEAR ME.

WE EMBRACED AWKWARDLY
AND KISSED EACH OTHER SOFTLY
AND THE KISS WAS ELECTRICALLY CHARGED
BUT CHASTE.

YOU GAVE ME A TURQUOISE FRIENDSHIP RING.

Cape Cod Morning

I sit at a table with a cup of strong coffee
in my hands
and watch through the open sliding glass door
as a mist slides along the point where sand meets surf.

The mist is obscuring
then revealing vistas of such enormous beauty
that my eyes get moist with tears because
seeing these vistas almost hurts.
It appears as if the horizon is endless.
I feel small in comparison.

There are people walking up and down the beach
braving a cool summer wind that blows with an eerie nonchalance
across the sand dunes.

The People walking along the beach
do not seem to mind the wind whipping their hair
and blowing their hats away.
I feel that there is a sense of unnerving stillness
And peacefulness
growing and manifesting itself in my psyche
these feelings I hope will remain present in my being for a long
time to come.

I now feel the tensions of life
slipping away to be replaced with the stillness and peacefulness
as I watch the winds pick up and scurry along the beach to
find rest in the high dunes.

I can feel myself smiling with every sip of my coffee.

I need for this sense of calm to stay with me for a little while.
I need some quiet and calm in my life or I will scream.
I do not want to leave but my phone rings and life is
calling me back.

Dancing on Bretton Point

in THE LATE SUMMER OF 2002
It was early in the evening when
she said

"I want to take you to my favorite spot in NEWPORT".
"Where is that?" I said
We arrived at BRETTON POINT about an hour later.

We got out of the car.

The radio was playing.
She turned up the volume.
A song by DON HENLEY called THIS LOVE CAME ON
THE RADIO
and we started to slow dance.
We danced holding each other close
There was a light summer wind.
The quiet, soft waves crashed into the shore with a
languorous intensity.

It was at this point that
I REALIZED THAT SHE WAS TO BECOME THE
LOVE OF MY LIFE.
That was MANY years ago and I have never looked back
with anything but a feeling of deep and abiding love.
Of course,
like any other couple we have times of trouble and times of trial,
but it all has made our bond impregnable.
Nothing can come between us.
We are an us and people we know are jealous of us

TIGRANUS LEVANTUS is a pseudonym of a
writer by the name of RONALD E. FRUSTAGLIA
from BOSTON, MASSACHUSETTS,
now living in RHODE ISLAND.